Bishop of Orléans

The Future Oecumenical Council

Bishop of Orléans

The Future Oecumenical Council

ISBN/EAN: 9783337125271

Printed in Europe, USA, Canada, Australia, Japan

Cover: Foto ©Lupo / pixelio.de

More available books at **www.hansebooks.com**

AUTHORIZED TRANSLATION,
WITH PAPAL BRIEF.

THE

FUTURE ŒCUMENICAL COUNCIL.

A LETTER

BY THE

BISHOP OF ORLEANS

TO THE CLERGY OF HIS DIOCESE.

TRANSLATED BY

HENRY S. BUTTERFIELD,

(Translator of "The Roman Catacombs," &c.)

AND

E. ROBILLARD.

LONDON:
R. WASHBOURNE, 18A, PATERNOSTER ROW
1869.

R. Washbourne, Printer, 18a, Paternoster Row.

NOTICE.

In presenting the public with an English version of the Bishop of Orleans' *Lettre sur le Future Concile Œcumenique*, we have to append the following translation of the Brief which our Most Holy Father has been graciously pleased to address to His Lordship on the subject:—

"PIUS P.P. IX.

"Venerable Brother, Health and Apostolic Benediction.

"It is with very great pleasure, Venerable Brother, that We have seen you avail yourself of the opportunity offered by the Apostolic Letters addressed by Us to the Bishops of the Eastern rite not in communion with Us, as well as to the other non-catholic Christians, to give a new and more extended edition of your Letter on the Future Œcumenical Council, on that which is to be its character and cause its utility. And We congratulate you on having stated with as much clearness as eloquence the sound doctrine on the rights and prerogatives of the Holy See, and on its supreme authority in these kinds of assemblies. You have also explained in a very pertinent and luminous manner what is Our solicitude for the salvation of those who are in error, and triumphantly demonstrated that the exhortations which have emanated from Us are inspired only by the spirit of charity, and have but one end—the glory of God, the progress of the Church, and the true interests of those to whom We address Ourselves. We have therefore received with gratitude your work, which We foresee and hope will cause the darkness, which ignorance and malignity have spread in minds, to disappear, and incline all hearts to desire the very efficacious remedy of the Council. This remedy has in past centuries dissipated errors and restored peace to troubled Christian society in the same manner, by making the causes of actual evils disappear, it will be able to avert the formidable calamities which threaten our times. Meanwhile, as a token of divine blessings and of Our very particular favour, receive the Apostolic Benediction, which from the depths of Our heart We bestow upon you and your Diocese.

"Given at Rome, from Saint Peter's, this 25th of November, in the year 1868, and the 23rd of Our Pontificate.

"PIUS IX, P.P."

This work, then, has won a costly prize—the approval and benison of the Vicar of Jesus Christ, and the addition of a word here were obviously needless.

But we cannot refrain from expressing the pleasure we have experienced, within the last few days, in learning from the illustrious Bishop himself, that not only has the original Letter already had an enormous circulation in France and elsewhere, but that translations have been very widely diffused throughout Italy, Spain and Germany.

Assuredly this tends to evince the interest that the Holy Father's act has awakened, and to prove that, amid the discordant cries and malicious comments of his foes—always uneasy in their "house built upon the sands"—multitudes are anxious to lend an ear to kindly words of explanation.

We trust, therefore, that in countries where the English language is spoken, the Bishop's work, which we have essayed to clothe to the best advantage in English garb, may meet with an equally favourable reception; and we pray that, by its means, Unity—ever hand in hand with her twin-sister, Peace—may proceed more prosperously on her way, "to the praise and glory of God's Holy Name, and to the benefit of all His Holy Church."

H. S. B.

January, 1869.

CONTENTS.

LETTER ON THE FUTURE ŒCUMENICAL COUNCIL.

The Church and the world, my Brethren, had already been waiting for a year in anxious expectation. Before the Catholic Bishops assembled at Rome for the Eighteenth Centenary of the Martyrdom of St. Peter and the solemn canonization of Saints, the Sovereign Pontiff had all at once proclaimed the necessity for an Œcumenical Council, and declared his resolution shortly to convoke it.

The Bull of Convocation has just appeared. On the 29th of June last, the Feast of the Holy Apostles Peter and Paul, the Holy Father, by letters addressed to all the Bishops of the Christian world, has fixed the date of the future Council, and summoned to Rome the Episcopate of the whole earth.

Since that period, by two truly paternal Letters, the Holy Father has successively invited the non-united Greek Bishops and our separated brethren of all the Protestant Communions to take advantage of the future Council, in order to resume the work of unity, several times already attempted by the Church, but interrupted by the misfortunes of the times.

So, it is no longer only a hope. The first act necessary for the holding of the Council, its canonical convocation, is accomplished; and the Apostolic Letters, already known to the whole world, and everywhere received with joy in the midst of the pre-occupations and gloominess of the present times, have made hearts thrill: looks are directed anew towards Rome: the indifferent, enemies themselves, attentive and astonished, feel that something grand is preparing.

And in fact, my Brethren, what is being prepared at Rome and in the Church is a rare and solemn fact, whose sovereign importance none can disown, and which will be, perhaps, the greatest event of the century.

Be not astonished at this language. I know that events of immense magnitude have marked the outset of the 19th century, and its stormy course; that great revolutions have passed over it, and that only yesterday we saw one of the oldest thrones of Europe overthrown; that conflagrations and wars have agitated nations; that formidable problems are set at the present time in the new and the old world. Yet, there is even in this century something superior to earthly ambition and the eager interests of political passions: it is the spiritual interests of nations, and those supreme questions whose solution is of consequence to the peace of souls and the eternal destiny of mankind.

It is on this account, my Brethren, that the Church—which appears so small an affair to certain men, and seems to them to occupy so little a place in our modern society, that we to-day hear politicians seriously advising one to take no further account of her—that the Church is and remains the noblest power in the world, because she is the spiritual Power, and Rome, the centre of that power, Rome, who soon will see within her walls those great assizes of Catholicity, will always be, in the words of her poet, the most beautiful and the most holy of things under the sun: *Rerum pulcherrima Roma.*

What is then, my Brethren, this Catholic Church, and what is this Council which in a few months is about to present so grand a spectacle to the world?

Following the example of many of my venerated colleagues, who have already in France and in different parts of Christendom published pastoral instructions on the subject, I come in my turn to discourse with you thereof. I will remind you what are Œcumenical Councils, to which we are long unaccustomed; I will tell you what motives, inspired from on high, have caused the Holy Father to decide upon this Act, the most extraordinary and important of the Pontifical Government; then we shall see if there be any foundation for the alarm which the announcement of such an act has given birth to in some malevolent or ill-informed minds; lastly, I will tell you what we Bishops, Priests and Faithful, have a right to hope.

I.

The Council.

"God," says Bossuet, "has performed in our midst a work, which, unconnected with every other cause, and depending from Him alone, fills up all times and all places, and bears all over the earth, with the impression of His hand, the character of His authority. That work is Jesus Christ and His Church."

There exists, then, in this world, above human things, yet intimately mixed up with them, a spiritual society, an empire of souls. This empire, of a peculiar and divine order, more of heaven than of earth, is nevertheless a true empire here below,—a complete society, having, like every other, its organization, laws, action and life; a society founded not by the hand of man, but by God Himself; requiring no human authority for its existence, for it has a mission as well as a sacred origin, and from them it derives all its essential rights: a traveller upon earth and a divine stranger, as Bossuet says again, nevertheless a sovereign, a sovereign of souls, over which it has inviolable jurisdiction; not encroaching upon human powers, but not abdicating its divine rights; happy to meet with their co-operation, and never rejecting their alliance, but knowing, if necessary, how to dispense with them; not disturbing their terrestrial mission, but unable to consent to her own being disturbed by them: a universal society which knows neither limits in time, nor boundaries in space; the depository of celestial goods, and charged to communicate to men till the end of time the truths of the Gospel, and by this mission, as by this origin and this expansion, holding in the world, civilized by it, a place that no other power can ever fill.

Yes, there is this marvel upon the earth: in the midst of all governments, human, temporal, limited, changeable, there is this spiritual Society, this government of souls, spread everywhere, immutable, boundless —the Church.

If we look more closely at her constitution—and we must cast at least a rapid glance at it, in order to understand well the most solemn of her acts, the Œcumenical Council—we shall see with what divine art Jesus Christ has proportioned the means to the end. The Son of God, it is our belief, has given to men, not for a time, but for the whole duration of time, *omnibus diebus, usque ad consummationem sæculi*, an entirety of truths, precepts and sacred institutions. Of these divine revelations the Christian Society, which our Lord called His Church, *Ecclesiam meam*, has the trust: a visible society, since religion should not be a hidden thing; perpetually visible, perpetuity having been promised to it; lastly, a universal society, since all men, without exception, are called and admitted to it.

But the trust of the divine revelations could not be transmitted through all ages without alteration, had it been abandoned to the variable and fanciful interpretations of private judgment. It was then indispensable that a doctrinal and sovereign, *i. e.* infallible, authority should be instituted; for an authority cannot be sovereign in matters of faith, and obtain interior assent, without being infallible. And this is what the Founder of Christianity has willed and done, when giving the apostles their mission He pronounced these words, the last which were uttered by his lips: "As my

Father has sent me, so also I send you. Going, therefore, teach all nations, baptizing them in the name of the Father, and of the Son, and of the Holy Ghost. Teaching them to observe all things whatsoever I have commanded you; and behold, I am with you all days, even to the consummation of the world."

Such then, is the essential character of the Church: she is a doctrinal authority, by the divine assistance providentially infallible in the things revealed of God.

Of infallibility, we know, is born unity; not a unity of accident and of fact simply, but a necessary and permanent unity, since the principle of unity is permanent in the Church. The principle, and moreover the centre of unity were in the nature of things, in the indispensable conditions of a Church thus founded. In fact, for this teaching Church, spread over the universe, a centre, a head, a chief was necessary to form her in one and the same body. In this necessity Jesus Christ did not fail, and He chose amongst His apostles one whom He invested with special privileges, and to whom He confided, according to His Divine expression, *the keys of the kingdom of Heaven*, whom He established as the basis, the foundation stone of the edifice, whom He charged *to confirm his brethren in the faith*, whom He named *the pastor of the sheep* as well as *of the lambs*, that is to say, Pastor and Chief of the whole fold.

This is the Hierarchy of the Church. In order to be a perpetual contradiction to time which destroys everything, and to render the assistance necessary to the human mind which is incessantly changing, a religious society thus constituted was required. But a divine hand was also required to establish thus a society composed of men; and this great character of authority and unity, in perpetuity and universality, is stamped upon the Church as the glorious impression of the powerful hand that founded her. Thus she dwells amongst men constant amidst universal inconstancy. In vain will the natural restlessness of the human mind run foul of all her dogmas, and heresies succeed heresies:* that inevitable commotion will be unable to do aught against her firm constitution, and she will remain, as the apostle says, the pillar and ground of the Truth: *Columna et firmamentum Veritatis.*†

Such is the Catholic Church.

Well, my Brethren, an Œcumenical Council is this Catholic Church assembled to do more effectively the work, which, dispersed over the world, she does every day, namely, the transmission to men, and the authentic interpretation, of the dogmatic and moral truths contained in authentic revelation.

And this, my Brethren, is what I now wish well to explain and make clear to our contemporaries, too unaccustomed to these things.

My design is not, however, you understand, to treat fully of Councils; volumes could be and have been written on this subject. But there are at least some necessary ideas about them, which it is essential should be stated with accuracy, since these matters are at this time little known, and, besides, in everything simple and fundamental ideas are the most useful.

A Council, then, is an assembly of Bishops met to treat of faith, morals and discipline.

A Council is particular or general; particular, if it represent only a part of the Church; general or œcumenical, if it represent the Church universal. A general Council, by reason of its representing the whole Church, has the privilege of doctrinal infallibility and supreme authority, given by Jesus Christ to the Church herself, to the body of pastors united to their Head: a particular Council has it not.

The supreme Head of the Church, the Pope, alone has the right to convoke general Councils.

For the same reason it is also to the Pope alone to whom belongs the right of presiding over them. In fact

* *For there must be also heresies* (1 Cor. xi. 19). "Terrible *must!*" says Bossuet somewhere.

† 1 Tim. iii. 15.

Œcumenical Councils have always been presided over by the Popes themselves or their Legates. Thus at Nice, Constantinople, Ephesus, Chalcedon, as well as at the Council of Trent, the Popes presided by their Legates. At the Councils of Lateran, Lyons, Vienna, Florence and Vienna, they presided in person.

"Most Holy Father," wrote the Fathers of the Council of Chalcedon to St. Leo, "in the midst of the Bishops, judges in matters of faith, you were presiding, as the Head over the members, in the person of those who represented you."*

In the same manner as it is the duty of the Sovereign Pontiff to convoke and preside over the General Council, is it for him to close, to dissolve, if necessary, and to confirm the same. Agreement of the Bishops with the Pope is manifestly necessary for the œcumenical issue of a Council.*

Gathered in Council from all parts of the world, with the Pope at their head, either in person or by his Legates, the Bishops decide questions, as witnesses of the faith of their Churches, as judges of the divine law. *Episcopis judicibus*, said the Fathers of Chalcedon immediately. *Definiens subscripsi; subscripsi pronuntians cum sanctâ synodo*, is how the Bishops signed at Chalcedon and Ephesus, and also at Trent.

Law has regulated the exterior forms of these assemblies. There are solemn *sessions* in which decrees are promulgated, and *congregations* in which they are elaborated—with what care, scruples, and inquiries the history of the Council of Trent attests, and of which the next Council of Rome will be a proof no less glorious.

The Pope, in fact, as soon as he had taken the great resolution of summoning a Council, has applied himself to it with an activity proportioned to the importance of the future assembly, and as becomes the

---

* *Episcopis judicibus, sicut membris caput, præeras in his qui tuum tenebant locum* (Epist. ad Leon. Conc. coll. R. t. ix., p. 204.)

part of the Head of the Church in an Œcumenical Council. Several commissions or congregations, composed of learned Cardinals and theologians chosen in every country, have been immediately appointed by him, and are busily engaged in preparing the matters which will be treated of in the Council. There is a special Congregation for Dogma; one for Canon Law; one for all that concerns the religious orders; one for the relations between Church and State; one for the Churches of the East.

It is the custom in the Church, when the Pope wishes to summon an Œcumenical Council, to inform beforehand with all solemnity the Bishops, who should bring to it, with the authority which from their character they enjoy, the counsel of their experience, and the light and special competency to understand the times and the wants of nations, which their dispersion throughout all the countries of the world gives them.

Therefore, since last year, Pius IX., in two allocutions addressed to the Bishops assembled in Rome, has announced to them the future Council; and by his last Bull he has just called them all to it, and fixed the precise date, in order that the Prelates, informed and summoned beforehand, should have time to study at leisure the questions, and arrive perfectly prepared for the time indicated by the Sovereign Pontiff.

I need not add that, if the Pope and Bishops assembled can carry out disciplinary laws and modify more or less in the Canon Law what is not by its nature immutable, the mission of Councils, in matters of faith, is not to make dogmas: dogmas are not made in Councils, but they are declared. What belongs to them and what they have always done, is to examine scripture and tradition, even as the authorized interpreters of scripture and tradition; and it is with the aid of all these assembled lights, after most searching debates, and after the assistance of the Holy Ghost has been long invoked, that the Council pronounces and defines, according to the necessities of the times and the wants of souls, what has been and what is the belief of the Church.

History counts to the present time eighteen Œcumenical Councils,* but it would be difficult to fix upon the infinite number of particular Councils. Nothing places in the light more than these conciliatory assemblies the powerful vitality of the Church and the strength which she carries within her to defend herself, either against the errors to which the human mind ceases not to give birth, or against the corruptions and abuses inevitable to the infirmity of human nature. It is the sole society upon earth in which revolutions are not necessary, and in which reforms are always possible. There is not one of these thousand Councils,

* The following is a list of these eighteen Œcumenical Councils: 1. *Nice*, in 325, against Arius, who denied the divinity of the Word; 2. *Constantinople*, in 381, against Macedonius, who attacked the divinity of the Holy Ghost; 3. *Ephesus*, in 431, against Nestorius, who erred concerning the Incarnation, and refused to give the Blessed Virgin the title of Mother of God; 4. *Chalcedon*, in 451, against Eutyches, who had flung himself into an error contrary to that of Nestorius; 5. *Constantinople*, in 553, against the three famous Chapters which prolonged the error of Nestorius upon the Incarnation; 6. *Constantinople*, in 680, against the Monothelites, who prolonged the error of Eutyches by denying that Jesus Christ had a human will; 7. *Nice*, in 787, against the Iconoclasts, or breakers of images; 8. *Constantinople*, in 869, against Photius, the author of the Greek schism; 9. *Lateran*, in 1123, for the promulgation of peace between the Priesthood and the Empire, after the long quarrels about Investitures, and for the Crusades; 10. *Lateran*, in 1139, for the re-union of the Greeks, and against the errors of the Albigenses; 11. *Lateran*, in 1179, for different questions of discipline, and against the heresies of the time, the Vaudois, &c.; 12. *Lateran*, in 1215, still against the same heretics; 13. *Lyons*, in 1245, for the Crusade and the strife with the Emperor Frederick; 14. *Lyons*, in 1274, for the Crusade and the re-union of the Greeks; 15. *Vienna*, in 1311, for the Crusade and divers questions of discipline, and for the affairs of the Knights Templars; 16. *Florence*, in 1439, for the re-union of the Greeks; 17. *Lateran*, in 1511, against the council of Pisa; 18. *Trent*, in 1545, against Protestantism. Many sessions of the Council of Constance are also regarded as œcumenical.

in fact, that has not decreed upon discipline at the same time as upon faith; and the great Council of Trent itself, without fearing that word "Reform," which had inflamed Europe, re-took it, because it belonged to it, and accompanied all its definitions of the faith with decrees upon reformation: *De reformatione*. Assembled in Œcumenical Council, the Pope and the Bishops examine with a steady gaze the whole situation of affairs in the Christian republic, and courageously bring a remedy for its wounds and sufferings. By it the immortal youth of the Church is renewed; a stronger and more vigorous breath is infused into that vast body, and society itself feels its blessed influence.

It is then, my Brethren, one of these œcumenical assemblies that the Pope has just convoked. After having deeply meditated upon the wants of the times, and long prayed to God, the Head of the Catholic Church has spoken one word; made one solemn sign, and it is enough: from East and West, North and South, from all points of the inhabited world, of every tribe, every language, every nation, the heads of that great spiritual society, all the dispersed members of that government of souls, who take their names from the first towns of the universe in which they are seated,—the Bishops are about to set out, and assemble in the place marked out by the Sovereign Pontiff, to treat, not as in human congresses, of peace and war, of conquests and frontiers, but of souls and their sacred interests, of things spiritual and eternal; to obey that divine saying which has founded the Church: *Euntes ergo, Docete omnes Gentes*; "Going, teach all nations;" to accomplish the most august duty of their sovereign mission; to proclaim in a general assembly of the Church, in face of human errors, the truths, the sacred trust of which has been confided to them by Him who is Truth itself. Such is the work of an Œcumenical Council; is there on earth a greater work?

It is three hundred years since the world has seen these assemblies, and even at the commencement of this century, people believed them impossible. "In modern times," wrote J. de Maistre, not fifty years ago, "since the civilized universe has been, so to say, minced by so many sovereignties, and immensely enlarged by our hardy navigators, an Œcumenical Council has become a chimera."

People remembered the political difficulties which so sadly fettered the Council of Trent, and the present times appeared still more unfavourable: they thought modern powers more defiant and hostile, and the liberty of the Church more shackled, her action more than ever lessened. But they did wrong to calumniate our times; and in lieu of defying Providence, we shall do better to admire His powerful hand, which, as the ancient proverb said, *Writes straight upon crooked lines*, and forces events to give way, in spite of man, to His eternal designs. As a missionary and traveller, the Church wants to see roads shortened. As a preacher and deliverer, she profits and rejoices at the falling away of all obstructions. Now our age has accomplished these two works, the doing away of distances, the lowering of barriers—I mean distances and barriers in the political and social sense, as well as in a material point of view. People have thought to serve their interests thereby: they have served faith: and all that stir which seemed to be made in a sense opposed to the Church's, and against Her, turns to her profit. The spirit of modern times obliges governments, whether they will or not, to be more equitable towards the Church, and causes the old prejudices, which but lately still impeded her action, to disappear; and behold, the holding of an Œcumenical Council is, politically, easier to-day than it would have been in the times of Philip II., Louis XIV., or Joseph II.

"Only to convoke all the Bishops," said De Maistre again, "and to establish legally this convocation, five or six years would not suffice." And to-day it suffices Pius IX. to cause his Bull to be affixed to the walls of the Lateran! Modern publicity, in spite even of contrary wills, carries it to the extremities of the world; soon, thanks to the marvellous progress of science and industry, upon the wings that steam lends our vessels, and upon the chariots of fire which consume space, from continents, in direction the most contrary, from islands the most distant, the Bishops will come at the appeal of the Pontiff. They will come from free countries, and, we hope, from those which are not; and thus, I love to repeat it, that double current of the ideas and the industry of our time is about to be of use, not only to material life, but to the government of souls, to the highest manifestation of the spiritual life in mankind, to the greatest work of the Spirit of God upon earth.

How just it is, since Providence has so willed, that, by this secret harmony hidden in the depths of things and in the unity of the divine work, matter will have been placed once more at the service of spirit; the thoughts of men at the disposition of the counsels of God!

Three times already, my Brethren, as you know, some years since, the Catholic Bishops have been enabled to assemble round the Vicar of Jesus Christ: but none of these three great meetings had the character of a Council. The glory of renewing the ancient traditions of the Church, so long interrupted, by the holding of a veritable œcumenical assembly, was reserved for this magnanimous Pontiff, so strong in his gentleness, so perfectly cheerful in his trials, and so confident in God who sustains him, and who has manifestly inspired him for the work of the Council.

II.

The Programme of the Council.

And why, with what thoughts, does the Head of the Church summon to these assizes of Catholicity those whom he calls "his venerable Brethren, all the Bishops of the Catholic world, whom their sacred character calls to share his solicitude?" *Omnes venerabiles fratres totius Catholici orbis sacrorum antistites, qui in sollicitudinis nostræ partem vocati sunt.*

The Apostolic letter tells us clearly; we must read it, and judge the Church fairly, on her own words, and not on rancorous or fruitless comments. This is how the Holy Father traces out in his Bull the programme of the future Council:—"This Œcumenical Council, then," says the Pope, "will have to examine with the greatest care, and to determine what it is best to do, in these times, so difficult and so hard, for the greater glory of God, for the integrity of the Faith, for the beauty of Divine Worship, for the eternal salvation of men, for the discipline of the clergy, regular and secular, for their salutary and solid instruction, for the observance of the ecclesiastical laws, for the reformation of morals, for the Christian education of youth, for general peace and universal concord.

"It will also be necessary to work with all our might, God aiding us, to remove every evil from the Church and from Society, to lead back into the right path of truth, justice and salvation, those unhappy ones who have wandered; to repress vice, and to repulse error, in order that our august religion and its salutary doctrines may acquire new vigour throughout the whole world; that it may be propagated daily more and more; that it may recover its empire, and that thus piety, honesty, justice, charity and all the christian virtues may thrive and flourish for the greater welfare of human society."*

---

* "In Œcumenico enim hoc Concilio ea omnia accuratissimo examine sunt perpendenda, ac statuenda, quæ hisce præsertim asperrimis temporibus majorem Dei gloriam, et fidei integritatem, divinique cultus decorem, sempiternamque hominum salutem, et utriusque Cleri disciplinam, ejusque salutarem, solidamque culturam, atque ecclesiasticarum legum observantiam, morumque emendationem, et christianam juventutis institutionem, et communem omnium pacem et concordiam in primis respiciunt. Atque etiam intentissimo studio curandum est, ut Deo bene juvante, omnia ab Ecclesia, et civili societate amoveantur mala, ut miseri errantes ad rectum veritatis, justitiæ, salutisque tramitem reducantur, ut vitiis, erroribusque eliminitatis, augusta nostra religio ejusque salutifera

The whole programme, the whole work of the future Council are in these words. There will then be two great objects in it, *the good of the Church and the welfare of human Society.* There will be that, and that only.

Before all, the Church assembles to re-animate her interior life, and as the Apostle says, *to stir up the grace of God which is in us.* It is the Church, my Brethren, who has this admirable privilege that I speak of: she is the only body which is endowed with this power of a perpetual growing-young-again in the midst of a perpetual existence. In virtue of her divine constitution, nothing changes in the truths which she guards, nothing is created, nothing lost, not a syllable, not an iota! *Iota unum, aut unus apex non præteribit,** says Jesus Christ. But, as a living institution, composed of men, borrowing her chiefs and her members from all nations, all ranks, always open to all who wish to come to her, and unceasingly being increased by new races,—as a river which receives rivulets into its midst reflects the objects on its banks, and adapts its course to climates, places and declivities,—the Church has the gift of accommodating herself to the times, the institutions and wants of the generations which she traverses, and to the centuries which she civilizes.

Further, she is here below perpetually labouring to make herself more worthy to speak to men of God, and her manner of doing so heard and understood. She examines without ceasing, with respect, but with sovereign authority, her disciplinary books, her laws, her institutions, her works, and especially her members distributed in the different degrees of the hierarchy.

Certainly we do not believe ourselves faultless or stainless. "What, are we astonished," said Fénelon

---

doctrina ubique terrarum reviviscat, et quotidie magis propagetur, et dominetur, atque ita pietas, honestas, probitas, justitia, caritas omnesque christianæ virtutes cum maxima humanæ societatis utilitate vigeant et efflorescant."

* St. Matth. v. 18.

formerly, "to find in man the remains of humanity!" But, eternal thanks to God! we possess in the imperishable treasure of truth and the divine laws, whose depositaries we are, the means of ever acknowledging our faults and reforming ourselves.

It is then against us, or rather, it is for us above all that the Council meets. There will not be a single one amongst us, who, coming to take his seat in that august Assembly, will not that morning have genuflected upon the last step of the altar, bowed his head, beaten his breast and said to himself: "If God be not better known, better served around me, if truth suffer violence, if the poor be not assisted, if justice be in danger, O God, it is through my fault, through my fault, through my most grievous fault!" Kings of the earth, who dispose, sometimes with such dreadful freedom, of the fate of nations, ah! how good for you also would such an examen be, if you could endure it! O human assemblies, parliaments, tribunals, popular conventions, do you think that that strict survey of oneself, those avowals, those scruples and those courageous habits of discipline and reform, will be useless to appease blind agitations and arrogant passions, or to shake off sleepy routine?

Everyone of us, then, having examined, interrogated and accused himself severely, will ask himself what are to-day the obstacles to the propagation of the Faith amongst nations who have not received it, to its re-establishment amongst those who have lost it? We shall revise regulations; we shall reform abuses; we shall re-establish forgotten laws; we shall modify that which requires it. Under the supreme authority of our common Father, the Bishop of bishops, the experience of the old men, the ardour of the younger, the inspiration of the holiest, the wisdom of the wisest,—all will concur to this generous and sincere verification of our proper state, our mission on earth and our duty; and this examen will be made in the freest and most brotherly discussion, and be ere long followed by sound resolutions, which will henceforth and for ever become the rule of our life.

Such, then, will be the first object of the assembly of the Bishops: a sublime and humble object, which the children of the Church respectfully admire, and which strikes her enemies themselves with a wonder that they in vain seek to disguise. Aye, our ministry is so beautiful, our assemblies are so elevated above others, that the language of men contains the involuntary avowal of that superiority. For when they wish to define a noble function, a superior mission, a *rôle* apart, they call it, often indeed with exaggeration, a *Priesthood;* and if they wish to speak of a solemn and imposing meeting, which will leave a mark in history, they say, "it is as a *Council* of kings or of legislators." Without having to puff ourselves up, Priests or Bishops, human language has no words more exalted; for our hands have not done these things; they come from God, and the haughtiness of the words which expresses them, recalls to our humility, with the majesty of our vocation, the formidable extent of our duties.

But, finally, why, in our days, at this present time, this retreat of the whole Catholic episcopate to the privacy of a new "upper chamber!" Why, if I may venture so to speak, this holy watching of arms? Why these preparations, all this machinery and work of a great Council? Why, by the inspiration and under the eye of God, has the Sovereign Pontiff judged it expedient to meet at this moment, in this second half of the 19th Century?

It is said of our Master, the Divine Saviour of the world: *Vulneratus est propter iniquitates nostras.* Now it is for men's iniquities, and for ours, that we are about to impose upon ourselves so many labours. The more difficult the times, the more it behoves us to be pure in the presence of more formidable trials, armed for sharper struggles, and wise on the eve of hotter discussions. And if men ask us why we are about to strive thus to augment light and charity in our midst, we would answer that, without forgetting ourselves and our wants, we do it on their account also, contemplating their state, their aspirations and their sufferings, and in the desire to do them more good.

III.

The Causes of the Council.

What is then to-day the condition of the souls, and the state of the nations spread over the face of the earth? Who is not pre-occupied therewith?

The Pope, casting a glance upon the world, and lending from afar an ear to the commotions of contemporary society, has been unable not to see, as all do (he says), the great crisis, or, as the Bull expresses it, the tempest which at this time agitates the Church and Society: *Jam vero omnibus compertum exploratumque est qua horribili tempestate nunc jactetur Ecclesia, et quibus quantisque malis ipsa affligatur Societas.* What is, my Brethren, this crisis in the Church and the world?

If you embrace in your view the sequel of history, and that vast ocean of ages upon which we are borne for an instant, and then swallowed up in our turn, you will answer at once, It is certain that this crisis is but an incident of the perpetual crisis, a scene of the uninterrupted drama, which composes the destiny of humankind. Inexperienced passengers always believe that they have embarked in foul weather, and imagine that the sea has rocks and waves only for them. But old sailors well know that the tide is ever uncertain, and that the tempest of the day which is breaking has been preceded by other tempests.

And if we are just as well as attentive, we shall acknowledge moreover that this crisis of the present time does not occur by chance, and escapes no more than others the direction of God. I would even say, in considering the deep designs of Providence, that this crisis is not without grandeur, and that it has its beauty, its laws and its end, as the phenomena of nature in appearance most confused and disorderly. Through the struggles and obstacles unceasingly renewed, the Church, who knows whither she goes, and men, often unknown to them, pursue the ideal of the Gospel; and the Church, whose mission it is to elevate the soul thereto, laments here below because this ideal is never sufficiently realized for the happiness and glory of mankind. No doubt we must acknowledge the efforts of labour, intelligence and courage which men now display; there have accumulated for some centuries treasures of science, riches and power, and there has arisen in the two worlds a surprising crop of men of talent, artists and orators, scholars and military men, administrators and *literati*, whose names and whose labours will be saluted by posterity with legitimate gratitude. But all that suffices not for mankind; and having been just towards the good, let us be just towards the evil; let us look our century itself in the face, and, with the august and veracious Pius IX., let us agree that human society is at this moment deeply troubled.

Do not think, my Brethren, that I mean to speak here of the troubles of politics and war.

I know that Europe has more than once resounded, in these last years, with the din of battle, and that at this hour a secret disquiet still agitates the mind; nations are arming and preparing themselves, one would say, for gigantic shocks. Is it of these powerful political interests—these questions of nationalities, of equilibrium and of frontiers—that the Pontiff wishes to speak? No doubt the Church is not indifferent to peace or war amongst nations, and indeed her prayers ascend daily to heaven for concord amongst princes and Christian nations. But in truth, I think I have said so already, it is not to settle such questions that she gathers her Council: the pacific assembly convoked to Rome will meditate neither revolutions nor conquests, neither leagues of nations or sovereigns, nor the raising or overthrow of dynasties. Whilst all Europe, and, if we cast a look further, whilst the new world, like the old, are trembling at the sound of war or revolutions, there, at Rome, in that august centre, in that reserved place, gathered near the Successor of Peter round the chair of truth, the pastors of the people, their feet upon the earth and the immovable rock, but their eyes towards heaven, will occupy themselves with souls, with the wants of souls, with the eternal salvation of souls, in a word, with the superior and permanent interests of mankind.

And surely they will do well; for, (who can hide it?) are not souls in danger, and is not the faith of nations menaced?

What new heresy, then, has sprung up? you will say to me. What new heresy, my Brethren? From the bosom of the Church, none; never has the clergy been more united in the faith, from one end of the world to the other. Outside the Church, on the contrary, not only are the same attacks, a hundred times repulsed, a hundred times renewed, reproduced under new forms and in fresh wrath against all points of the Christian doctrine, more than this; but, with an impiety which surpasses that of the 18th century, natural truths themselves—those primordial truths upon which everything here below rests—are denied and audaciously discussed. Science also has its heresies; there is a schism amongst philosophers; and reason submits in her turn to the assaults which appeared reserved for the Faith. Strange! It is the Faith which keeps to-day the treasures of reason, and serves it for a rampart. It is you, to-day, O scholars, O thinkers, it is you who want us! You accuse us every day of having neither science nor intelligence, but you, my poor brothers, so learned, so intelligent, have not nearly known how to keep a single durable truth! And you who wished to reform the Church, O Protestants, you it is, to-day, who have need of reform, and who feel how the benefit of authority is wanting in you.

See, in fact, the state of intellect. Whither go, from all parts, the separated philosophies? For three centuries, in that Germany, which to-day is so severely knocked about and shaken, violent spirits have sprung up, who, rejecting the bridle of faith, and giving themselves up to all the temerities of thought, have exhibited to the astonished world all the audacities, and at the same time all the weaknesses of reason, ere long followed, as ever, by audacities and weaknesses of conduct. From these prodigious efforts of mind and erudition, what has emanated? The resurrection of all the ancient errors, pantheism, atheism, scepticism, and even in religion the most contradictory caprices of an exegesis by which all Christianity would perish: this is where have ended, under our eyes, eighteen centuries after Jesus Christ, the greatest intellectual labours perhaps of which the world has been witness.

And to-day, amongst us, what do you see? A breach made in religious convictions, the dissolution of all faith, even philosophical, the overthrow of all rational truth; and the invasion of a pretended science infatuated with itself, which disowns reason and wishes, by the name of materialism and atheism, to snatch from men faith in an immortal soul and belief in God. By means of the press,—journals, pamphlets, novels,—most fatal doctrines concerning God, the soul, morals, the future life, the family and society, are zealously spread abroad. Many of our contemporaries either sink in these errors or float, without compass and without guide, at the mercy of all the winds of doubt: on all sides men's minds are wrapt in the darkness of a tempest which penetrates to the very depths of the popular masses.*

---

* When, two years ago, I published "Athéisme et le Péril Social," and more recently "Alarmes de l'Episcopat," writings in which I denounced the efforts of atheism and contemporary impiety, some persons appeared to doubt, in spite of the positive proofs accumulated by me, that the evil had made so much progress, and also that impious doctrines could have social consequences so disastrous. Now, since this, the progress of irreligion has been so rapid, that to-day the evil bursts forth on all sides.

At the same time, great misunderstandings have arisen on all questions which concern the Church, and, by consequence, war is eagerly waged against her. When there burst forth in France the Revolution

---

There have been held this year, in Europe, three principal international congresses of workmen, at Brussels, Nuremberg and Gênes. What have we heard in these congresses? Cries of impiety and social war War to God! War to governments! War to capital!

The "International Association of Workmen," gathered together in congress at Brussels, a congress formed by delegates of the workmen's associations which cover Europe, said in its Report:—

"To-day man has at length been enabled to recognize his true and only enemy; in politics, this enemy is called THE LAW, symbolized by the MONARCH; in morals, GOD, symbolized by the priests and the Popes; in political economy, the INEQUALITY OF CONDITIONS, symbolized by MONEY." (Quoted by the *Univers* of the 3rd October, 1868.)

But what it is well to know is, that this International Association of Workmen, born only four years ago, has already branches all over Europe, and even in America. I read, in fact, in the speech of the President (sitting of the 6th September):—

"In America the workmen have organized and affiliated themselves ...... They count upon soon taking possession of the legislative power, which belongs actually to the citizens.

"In England the *fall of classes* is equally commenced, and is pursued with success.

"In Germany and Switzerland the Association equally makes progress. One hundred and twenty workmen's associations are at this moment assembled at Nuremberg.

"The ideas of the association also make way in Italy."

We have just seen what these ideas were; the same President, in the same sitting, thus exposed them:—

"The paid workman is as unhappy as was once the negro of America ...... Still more unhappy.

"There is inevitably war between workman and master.

"The workman should to-day become his own master."

And the President thus concludes his speech:—"In our former congresses we have discussed our theories; to-day we must act."

And the one hundred and twenty workmen's societies assembled at Nuremberg have, to be sure, expressed their adhesion to the congress of Brussels.

And, perfectly skilled in the means, the workmen of the Congress of Gênes have resolved to found *schools for the instruction of the people, but schools without religion*, according to the method of the educational leagues which are so actively being organized in France

which is making the circuit of Europe and of the world, the Church, attached to the old political order by ties made by time, was carried with it into the tempest, and people knew not how to distinguish in

---

at the present time, and which people, who do not see at all, pretend are inoffensive.

When I quoted that frightful explosion of materialism and atheism which took place two years ago at the congress of students at Liége, and those cries of impiety and savage barbarity—

"War to God! Down with the privileges of citizens! Down with capitalists!

"Revolution is the triumph of man over God!......

"The vault of heaven must be smashed like a ceiling of paper!...

"If property makes an obstacle to revolution, it is necessary, by the people's decrees, to annihilate property!......

"If a hundred thousand heads make an obstacle, they must fall! We have love only for collective humanity!"

When I quoted those words and many others, the most respectable of the impious journals have thought to answer by saying to us: "They were children!"

Well, are they children, those 2000 individuals here, and those 3000 there, who are gathering together at this moment in Paris? For there one cannot pronounce the name even of *God*, or that of *Jesus Christ*, nor mention the *Christian faith*, without provoking the most violent storms; so much so, that at one of these meetings, an orator having forgotten himself so far as to say, *God forbid!* the expression excited such clamour that the speaker was obliged to leave the platform; and in another meeting, another having simply said, *Dating from ......Jesus Christ* , also descended from the platform amidst a tumult, and at the effect of menacing cries.

But I have not heard say that they made descend from the platform him who said lately, "Frugality is one of the forms of assassination."

There is nothing, even to charity, which has not been there scorned and banished. The President, having proposed a collection for the victims of the horrible accident at Metz—the powder explosion—the assembly refused, because it would have been from charity; and *charity*, cried out an orator, is *a Catholic and not a democratic essence.*

If things go on some time in this way, the world, one can predict without being a prophet, will see catastrophes such as it has never seen.

I said one day, in a work, that some doctrines would lead us to barbarism. I have been reproached for this word. Well, *barbarism;* they do not defend themselves from it any longer; they make a show of it. I received, this morning even, the prospectus of a new "ATHEISTIC *(materialiste)* AND LITERARY" journal, which is going

the struggle made against her, what held to a state of things legitimate, without being necessary, and what constituted the essential principles and immutable spirit of Christianity. Hatred, blind and implacable, has amongst certain men survived; forgetting eighteen centuries of benefits, they have continued an ungrateful war; and as the tide of revolution in its course rolls up pellmell truths and errors, virtues and crimes, benefits and disasters, the Church, who never covenants with error and evil, persists in pointing out to the men of the period the delusion of deceptive words, and the dangers of false doctrines. Let us say all; because they are obstinate in charging the Church with thoughts and pretensions which are not hers, an impious or misled press blasphemes against the Church, and seeks to excite nations against her; and in make-believe, writless congresses, in the writings of journalists who inspire them, amidst the cries of social warfare, we hear blasphemies, at once stupid and sanguinary, against the Church; and we even see carried to the bosom of our legislative assemblies this causeless antagonism, in the name of which men are demanding a violent separation of the Church and society.

---

to appear at Paris precisely under that name, LE BARBARE ("The Barbarian"), and declares itself founded for the triumph of atheism. That prospectus professes that Robespierre was but behind-hand and reactionary, and that the Revolution has only come to its *apogee* with the *atheism* of the commune of Paris, *with the acts of accusation (réquisitoires) of Chaumette*, with *the witty and profound journal of Hébert.**

Now, I ask, is it a dream about atheism and the social danger? Was I wrong in seeing in those young atheists the *Héberts* and *Chaumettes* of the future?

* I would remind the English reader that it was Chaumette who, in conjunction with Hébert, originated the Feasts of Reason during the French Revolution. It would be impossible to conceive greater monsters. It was they who contrived the infamous accusation brought against Marie Antoinette on her trial. Chaumette proposed a moving guillotine to shed blood with profusion—in fact, every description of cruelty it is possible to imagine. Both perished miserably by the guillotine, blaspheming to the end.—H. S. B.

And lately, when the voice of the Sovereign Pontiff raised itself to point out the overflowing of the impious or immoral theories which inundate us, still what clamorous, what unmerited accusations resounded from all sides! Without understanding his language, they calumniated him; and we saw with grief politicians, under the effect of precipitate emotion, and without asking or waiting for necessary explanations, hasten also to proclaim an antagonism which, thank God, does not exist.

These hostilities against the Church, by alienating from her the nations which are seduced, render still more formidable the danger in which contemporary errors entangle us; for the doctrines are not inoffensive, and it is a law of history, confirmed by constant experience, that M. de Bonald promulgated when he wrote these strong words: "There are always great disorders where there are great errors, and great errors where there are great disorders." These are the ideas which give birth to facts; it is from on high that storms come.

And I ask men of integrity this: You have wished to found the government of nations and the conduct of life upon reason alone. For three-quarters of a century we have had experience of this. Where is it? Are morals better? Is authority firm? Is liberty founded? Has war disappeared? And misery? And ignorance? And these questions, which reason puts with a rare fertility of invention, but which she does not solve, these questions which touch upon the organization even of society, labour, wages, workmen, where are they? I exaggerate nothing in affirming that since reason pretends to reign alone, she reigns, as the evening star, over shades which she cannot conquer, and the earth has become, even in the most civilized society, an abode of disquiet, uneasiness, division, and dread. The nineteenth century is about to end agitated, weary, sterile, unmistakeably diseased. Very bold must he be who would dare affirm that it will end in glory and not in abysses.

IV.

Retrospect of the Past.

Nevertheless, I beseech my friends and brethren in the Faith to exaggerate nothing. It is allowable to be sad, in the face of the present hour, I repeat; and I should esteem a heart rather heedless that would not so feel. The men of my age, sons of the nineteenth century, have had beautiful dreams; we had nourished generous hopes; we are about to die, and to die deceived. But what! Is our short life all history? We did not live in the sixteenth century, we shall not live in the twentieth; but the Church was living yesterday, and she will live to-morrow. If I had to say what I hope, all my prophecies would not be lugubrious, and if I question it upon its recollections, the present time would gain by being compared with the past. In fact, let us again turn our looks towards the times that are no more: shall we see many centuries that had not their miseries and their perils? Ah! before the discouragements of certain Catholics, I call to mind that saying of one of the Books of Wisdom: *Ne dicas: Quid putas causæ est quod priora tempora meliora fuêre quam nunc sunt? Stulta est enim hujuscemodi interrogatio*; "Say not: what thinkest thou is the cause that former times were better than they are now? for this manner of question is foolish."*

I was re-reading recently the Bulls of Convocation of the ancient Councils of the Middle Ages: the lamentations of the Popes at the misfortunes of their epoch surpass the most dreadful that could be made heard at the present time. And not to go back beyond the Council of Trent, let the Church tell us of those times, for she was of them. What did she see then?

A century similar enough to our own, by the taste for letters and the revival of art; similar also by the bad

---

* Ecclesiastes vii. 11.

use of its gifts. The sixteenth century was peopling America, lately discovered; was there giving itself up to monstrous excesses of avarice and cruelty, and introducing the disgrace of slavery. It was receiving treasures from it, and turning them to the corruption of morals. If we look at thrones and into the bosom of nations, and even as far as the Church herself, the spectacle is yet very sad. That century has seen Henry VIII, Elizabeth, Christiern II, Yvan the Terrible, the Médicis, Charles IX and Henry III. That century has seen the sack of Rome and the siege of Paris. That century has seen the pretended Reformation rend the Church, unsettle Europe, cut in twain Christendom. When one reads the lives of the great and holy personages of that time, such as Dom Barthélemi des Martyrs, St. Charles Borromeo or St. Francis de Sales, what revelations of the evils in the Church and in society! I have recalled the Bulls of the Popes of the Middle Ages: read but those of the Pontiffs who convoked the Council of Trent, and you will see if Adrian VI, Paul III, Pius IV, did not utter cries respecting the perils of the Christian republic more alarming than those of Pius IX. Relaxations, disorders, scandals; a clergy ill-formed, religious orders debased; and then princes divided, nations trodden upon, war every day, in all countries. And to speak only of the Council, assembled in conjectures so sad, it was necessary to gather it in a little town hidden amongst the mountains of Tyrol, to await for six years the pleasure of princes, to suspend it, to resume it, and to submit to incessant and unjust contests.

But, vain obstacles! the power of the Church triumphed over all; and after the Council, suddenly, what a spectacle! What great men and what great works issued precisely from that Council, and from the regenerating breath it had caused to pass over Christian Society! St. Charles Borromaco, St. Philip Neri, St. Peter of Alcantara, St. Teresa, St. John of the Cross, St. Francis of Sales, St. Jane of Chantal,

St. Vincent of Paul, St. Francis Borgia and St. Francis Regis, inheritors of the spirit of St. Ignatius, and St. Francis Xavier; then, in train of the canonized Saints, the apostolic men who regenerated the people, Blessed Pierre Fourrier, Cardinal de Bérulle, M. Olier, M. Eudes, M. Bourdoise, Abbé de Rancé and so many others; then those multiplied congregations, those fruitful institutions which cause the clerical and religious life to re-blossom, and encourage everywhere study, regularity, charity; all that regenerating movement, in fact, for which the Church has laboured; then Bossuet, Fénelon, and the majestic unity of the 17th century. And in spite of all the abysses that this immortal mother of men has had to leap, the Church has now temples at Jerusalem, liberty at Pekin and Constantinople, the episcopal hierarchy in England and the Low Countries, Councils at Baltimore, Missionaries in Africa, in Oceania and Japan; she rejoices from the bottom of her heart to behold in all places, spite of all that religion has yet to long for, and all that she deplores, laws more equitable, armies less oppressive, the weak better protected, the poor better assisted, slaves set free. When she looks in the face the pretended reform which started up full of audacity, supported upon the politics of the 16th century, the Church to-day sees it doctrinally decaying, having travelled over its cycle and exhausted its arms. On the contrary, the Catholic Church, whose abuses, say they, could no longer be supported, presents herself with a Pope whose eminent virtues force respect; with Bishops more numerous and zealous, with priests, pious, united, devoted; with Orders learned and virtuous, re-tempered in persecution and poverty. And when this Church wishes to assemble a Council, it is to Rome herself that she summons it, with the help of an immense publicity, safe roads, rapid conveyances, and facilities of all kinds, which she owes to the spirit, the equity and the resources of the present time.

People know well enough that I am not one of those

who shut their eyes and are silent respecting the evils of our epoch and the perils of souls. But neither do I wish to respond ungratefully to God's favours, and not to see the strength which He always procures His Church, and the facilities for good which He gives in the worst times. One must not forget, besides, that it is the duty of men in all times to struggle, and that each century has its task and its trouble. I pity, I execrate not the present time; I do not bereave nations of all hope, neither do I launch anathemas at princes: they are not all-powerful, and they should consider themselves surrounded with many difficulties. I pray, then, for them, as the Church does; and as well as my feeble voice can, I warn them; and of all, princes and peoples, I ask loyal and sincere co-operation in the great work of the Church, which is the sanctification and civilization of the world.

What ought especially to be to us, men of the present time, a subject to lament bitterly, are these three evils which to-day are at their worst; the ruin of faith, precipitated by the impious direction of scientific and philosophical studies; the dissoluteness of morals, accelerated by the thousand novel means of a corrupting propagandism; and, lastly, the unjust misunderstandings which the enemies of religion are pleased to perpetuate between the Church and modern nations. These are the three maladies to heal, if God please.

There are certain persons in whose eyes these three plagues are but the partial results of what is for them, in the present as in the past, the greatest of all plagues, revolution. I like not that vague ill-defined word, which starts up and grows larger at will, as a spectre; but what is very true is, that the evils of which I speak maintain in the bosom of society a division of mind, a contempt of God and of all authority, a pride and a hatred which threaten that society with a continual return to revolutions.

V.

The help offered by the Council.

This is then why, my Brethren, the Church, who is the friend of souls, and who was never indifferent to the evils of society, has been troubled. No doubt, the Church and society are distinct; but as they move side by side in this world, and enclose in their bosom the same men, they are necessarily jointly responsible in their perils and in their sorrows. And the Church wishes to meet together because she feels she can do much towards healing their common evils.

Here, however, let us still beware of exaggerating or of extenuating truth. Does it depend upon the Church to destroy all human evils? No. But in that great labour, in that severe struggle between good and evil, she has her part, an immense part, and she is about to perform it. Man is free, and does good freely; but he is assisted by divine grace, which aids without injuring his liberty; for, as the great Pope St. Celestine said: *Auxilio Dei liberum arbitrium non aufertur, sed liberatur.* Depository of celestial goods, the Church is man's divine assistant, and lends him, even in the temporal order, supernatural assistance. And if to-day the Church assembles and recollects herself, it is once more the better to accomplish her task, and to work more efficaciously and powerfully for the welfare of mankind.

"Who can doubt," cries out the Holy Father, "that the doctrine of the Catholic Church possesses the virtue not only of being able to serve the eternal salvation of souls, but also the temporal welfare of nations, their true prosperity, order and tranquillity? *Nemo enim inficiari unquam poterit catholicæ Ecclesiæ ejusque doctrinæ vim non solum æternam hominum salutem spectare, verum etiam prodesse temporali populorum bono, eorumque veræ prosperitati, ordini ac tranquillitati.*"

And who could call in question this social and

civilizing power of the Church ? "*Religion! religion!*" cried out lately an eminent statesman,* "*it is the life of mankind, in all places, in all times, save in certain days of terrible crises and disgraceful decadency.* Religion to restrain or to satisfy human ambition; religion to sustain or to appease us in all our griefs, those of our condition or those of our soul! Let not policy, even the strongest, the most just, flatter itself that it can accomplish such a work without religion. *The more lively and extensive the social movement, the less will policy suffice to direct shaken humanity. A power higher than earthly powers is necessary,* perspectives longer than those of life are needed—God and eternity are necessary."

The Holy Father also, after having recalled the beneficent influence of religion in the temporal order, proclaims anew the harmony, so often affirmed by him, between faith and reason, and the mutual help which, in the views of Providence, they are called upon to lend one to the other. "In the same manner," says he, "as the Church sustains society, does divine truth sustain human science; she strengthens the ground under its steps, and by preventing it from wandering, she favours its progress; *Et humanarum quoque scientiarum progressui ac soliditati.*"

Hearken well to those words, ye who vainly attempt to set up science in antagonism to the faith! The Head of the Church fears not science; he loves it, he extols it, and he calls to mind that Christian truths serve its progress and its solidity. The most illustrious scholars that have appeared on earth, Leibnitz, Newton, Kepler, Copernic, Pascal, Descartes, near whom our scholars, if their pride be not too blind, should feel very small, thought as he.

It is, adds the Pope, what the history of all times demonstrates with unexceptionable evidence: *Veluti sacræ ac profanæ historiæ annales splendidissimis factis clare aperteque ostendunt.* And this is the

* M. Guizot.

meaning of the well-known saying of Bacon: "A little knowledge takes us from religion: much knowledge brings us back to it." Science, in fact, carried to the height of excellence, embraces the whole of the truths, and discovers the entire order of them.

The presumptuous ignorance or blind passions of our epoch may forget it; but the greatest minds have always acknowledged this agreement between faith and science, this harmony between Church and society, and rejected that antagonism of recent date and contrary to the testimony of history and the interests of truth.

But, let us not here, my Brethren, leave room for attacks by equivocal expressions. What does the Church do to transform society? History responds, and prejudice alone can imagine phantoms of encroachments on the legitimate liberty of the human mind. The Council of Rome will be the nineteenth General Council, and the forty or fifty nations which will be represented there, have all been converted in the same manner; that is to say, brought from barbarism to civilization by the authority of the Word, by the virtue of the Sacraments, by the instruction of Pastors, by the examples of the Saints. Such are the ways of God and the action of the Church, sometimes seconded, more often combated, by human powers.

Instructress of souls, the Church makes use of the method of all good education, authority, and patience. Whilst one doubts, she affirms; one denies, she insists; one obscures, she enlightens; one divides, she unites; she repeats over and over again the same lessons, and what lessons! The true nature of God, the true nature of man, liberty and moral responsibility, the immortality of the soul, the sacred rule of marriage, the law of justice, the law of charity, the inviolability of rights and property, the duty of labour, the need of peace. This, always, everywhere, to all; to kings and shepherds, to the Greeks and to the Romans, to England and to France, to Europe and to Australia, under Charlemagne or before Washington.

The continuance of these affirmations, I venture to say, causes order in society and in minds as certainly as the rising of the same sun causes the order of the seasons and the prosperity of husbandry. O philosophers who disdain the Church, be frank; without her what would have become of the notion of the living God among nations? O Protestants, O Greeks, acknowledge that without the Church you would have seen the image of Jesus Christ effaced before your eyes! O moralists and politicians, without her, what would you have done with the family and the sanctity of marriage?

Well! what the Church of Jesus Christ has done, she is going to do again; what she has said, she is about to affirm anew; she will continue her life, her way, her work, in the same spirit of wisdom and charity; she will continue to infuse into human reason the great truths of which she is the guardian, and it is thus, alone thus, notably thus, that she acts upon society.

The religion of nations, it has been said, is all their morality. Now morality being the true source of good policy and good laws, all progress of a people consists in infusing more and more into private and public life the primordial principles of justice. Every nation then that shall advance in the Christian sense, will advance to progress, and every century which would fain solve against the Gospel the questions which distract mankind, will take a wrong direction, and go to destruction. Here again interrogate the past, and it will answer you. Who has expelled from the world pagan corruption, who has civilized savages by converting them? See the East when Christianity was flourishing there, and see it under the domination of Islam! The influence of Christianity upon civilization is as glaring a fact as the sun. But the principles of the Gospel are far from having bestowed all they possess, and even time will never exhaust them, because they are of infinite profundity.

Thus, although centuries have drawn from the Christian principle of charity, equality and fraternity of men, consequences which have changed the old world, all the social applications of this beautiful doctrine are far from being exhausted; and I consider it is even the proper mission of modern nations, to cause this fecund principle to penetrate more and more into laws and morals, and to draw from it political, economical, and social consequences, which will be the glory of this century, if it depart not from Christian paths. But it is the mission of the Church and her Councils to maintain the principles of the Gospel free from all interpretations which falsify them.

Therefore, every great manifestation of evangelical truth, every explanation of obscurities and mistakes, every good understanding between nations and Christianity, is a work of progress at once social and religious — and this is precisely the work of the Council. This is why the Church is about to make this great effort, and display, as the Holy Father says, all her strength, *ut omnes nostras magis magisque exaremus vires;* this is why the Catholic Bishops will come from all parts of the world to consult with their head: *Sua nobiscum communicare et conferre consilia.*

Vainly do you say in your unjust and ignorant prejudices, that the Church is old and that the times are new. The laws of the world are old also, and all the new inventions, of which you are justly proud, exist and succeed only by the application of those laws.

Ah! you do not know of what elements, at once pliant and resisting, her Divine Founder has formed the Church, and what an organization, at once stable and progressive, He has given her. Such are the profoundness and fecundity of her dogmas, such also is the expansive character of her constitution, that she can live under all political *regimes*, and will never be surpassed by any progress of the human society. Without altering anything in her symbol, she draws from her treasure, as our Lord says, from age to age, and according to the wants of the times, old and new things, *de thesauro suo profert nova et vetera:* and you will always find her ready to adapt herself to all great social transformations, and to follow mankind in all the phases of his existence. The Gospel is the light of the world, and always will be; and this is why, rest assured, the next Council will be a sunrise and not a sunset.

VI.

Ill-founded fears on the subject of the Council.

What do you fear, then, timid Catholics or suspicious politicians? Ah! let mankind rather rejoice at the magnanimous resolution of Pius IX.; for it should be for them who believe, as for them who have not the happiness of believing, a solemn hope. If you have the faith, you are well aware that the Spirit of God presides at such assemblies. Doubtless there will be men there, and possibly weaknesses in consequence. But there will also be there holy devotion, great virtues, exalted intelligence, pure and courageous zeal for the glory of God and the welfare of souls, an admirable spirit of charity, and, above all, a superior and divine power, and God, there as always, will accomplish His work.

"God," says Fénelon, "watches so that the Bishops may always assemble freely when necessary, that they may be sufficiently informed and attentive, and that no corrupt motive may ever influence against the Truth those who are its depositories. In the course of an examination there may be irregular proceedings. But God knows how to draw from them what pleases Him: He carries them to His own ends, and the conclusion infallibly comes to the precise point He has fixed." *

* 2e Instruction pastorale sur le Cas de Conscience, ch. II., art. 3; 2 Mar. 1705.

Had one even the misfortune of not being Christian, and of not recognizing in the Church the voice of God, in a human point of view simply, what can be more deserving of sympathy and respect than this grand attempt of the Catholic Church to labour, in that which concerns her, for the enlightenment and peace of the world? And what more august and venerable than the assembly of those seven or eight hundred Bishops come from Europe, Asia, Africa, the two Americas and the distant isles of Oceania, by their age, knowledge and virtues, the most authorized representatives of all the countries they inhabit, of all the men of the universe with whom they are in contact every day? a true Senate of Mankind. This is seen nowhere, but it will be seen at Rome. And, unless the senses be confused by most unjust prejudices, what cabals, what exaggerations, what fits of obstinacy are to be feared from a meeting of old men come from all parts of the globe, almost all unknown to each other, without other antecedent bond than community of faith and virtue? Where will you find upon earth a higher expression, a higher guarantee of wisdom, even a wisdom such as men understand?

I have heard say that modern times, through too much experience, tired of placing confidence in one man, have faith in assemblies. What assembly could present such a union of intelligence, of independence, such diversity in unity?

What are these Bishops? Read their mottoes:

In the name of the Lord!—I bring peace!—I wish for light!—I diffuse Charity!—I shrink not from Toil!—I serve God!—I know only Christ!—All to all!—Triumphing over evil by good!—Peace in Charity! etc.

As to them, they have lost their former names; they sign by the name of a saint and the name of a town. Their own name is buried, as that of the architect, in the first stone of the Temple. There is BABYLON and JERUSALEM. There is NEW YORK and

WESTMINSTER. There is EPHESUS and ANTIOCH. There is CARTHAGE and SIDON, MUNICH and DUBLIN. There is PARIS and PEKIN. There is VIENNA and LIMA. There is TOLEDO and MALINES, COLOGNE and MAYENCE And they are called, also, Peter, Paul, John, Francis, Vincent, Augustine, Dominic; by the name of the great men who have founded or enlightened nations by announcing to them the Gospel. They do not bear only names past and present, but moreover the names of the future. This one is at the Red River, the other at Dahomey: that one is at Oregon, the other at Natal, at Victoria, at Saïgon. We, whom they call men of the past, labour for the future. We labour for lands to-day without towns, and for peoples yet without names. We go further than science, beyond commerce; where we are alone, in advance of you. When we do not out-strip your travellers, we tread in their footsteps. And why? To make Christians; that is to say men,—nations. Of what, then, have you fear? In what can a Council give umbrage to you who entitle yourselves, with so lofty a confidence, men of progress, heralds of the future?

Would it be nationalities, countries, which would find themselves disturbed by the Council? How could nationalities be menaced or betrayed by men who represent all the known nationalities of the globe, who invoke them and who live by them for their own account, and for the defence of their own faith? Will the Bishops of Poland come to an understanding with the Bishops of Ireland for the ruin of nationalities and the oppression of countries? But is there one French Bishop, one English Bishop, a Bishop of whatever nation it may be, who yields to no matter whom in patriotism, who is not proud at being as good a Frenchman, as good an Englishman, as good a citizen as any one?

Have liberties more disquiets to conceive? What can they dread from men, who from the Catacombs to the massacre of the Carmelites have established

Christianity only at the sacrifice of their lives, and have only seen their blood flow when people were slaughtering liberty at the same time as the Church? Is it the Bishops of America who will unite with the Bishops of Belgium, Holland, and Switzerland in a plot against liberties? Will the Bishops of the East come to an understanding with the Bishops of France, and so many other European Bishops, to sing the benefits of despotism?

No, no; there is no truth in all these fears, and they would be but empty phantoms to be despised, were there not at the bottom of all this the crafty work of a hatred which here foresees good, and wishes at any price to hinder it. What will the Council do? I am not going to say: God alone knows at the hour in which I speak. But I can say that it is only a Council, because eighteen centuries of Christianity and civilization know and attest it. A Council is the moral power *par excellence*,—it is the noblest alliance of authority and liberty that the human mind could conceive, and I dare even affirm that it would never have conceived it all alone.

I have not to trace here the limits of liberty or power: neither have I to characterise at this moment schism or heresy, English or German Protestantism, nor the false orthodoxy of Russia; I will here say but a single word, which I shall enlarge upon by-and-bye; it is that if the Churches can again become sisters, and if men will again become brothers, they will never be able to do it more surely, more grandly, more tenderly, than in a Council, under the auspices and in the bosom of the Church, who is the true mother.

Is it the different currents of opinion, that you think to perceive in the Church, which disturb you? I should have some right in this case to wonder at your solicitude; but I wish to accept it as sincere, and I reply to you: How little you know the Church! Her enemies every day represent our faith as a crushing yoke, which keeps us immovable, and hinders us from thinking. And when they see us thinking freely, they wonder. But this is in the very conditions of the life of the Church, for the grandest development of ideas always takes place in her bosom. It is true we have an immutable symbol, and we are not like philosophers all abroad, who do but search and recommence their researches without end, who always put off every thing in question, who travel and never arrive. There are for us points gained, defined, upon which we no more dispute. And thus the Church has unshaken foundations, and is not an edifice in the air. And yet in the Catholic Church liberty also has its place. Our anchors are powerful and our perspectives without limit, for, beyond points defined, space is still immense. Even in dogma the Christian mind has a magnificent work to accomplish, and one which will continue without ceasing, because, as I was saying just now, our dogmas have a depth infinite as God himself, and Christian reason will always be able to draw them up from it without ever exhausting them.

Be not astonished, then, to see Catholics thinking freely outside defined points, and upon those complex and difficult questions, which the vague language of the disputants of the day does but obscure. The spirit of Christianity has been long defined by St. Augustine in these memorable words: *In necessariis unitas, in dubiis libertas, in omnibus caritas.* The course of ages has changed nothing thereof. Besides, I was saying just now and I recall it, the Council, precisely because it is Œcumenical, *i. e.*, composed of all the Churches of the earth, of Bishops living under all political constitutions, under all social *regimes*, excludes necessarily the predominance of a school, of a narrow and national spirit, and local prejudices. It is the great Catholic spirit, you may be sure, and not such or such particular ideas, which will inspire the decisions; and, whatever may be the special opinions of such or such a fraction, of such and such a school, the Council will cause true light and unity. Liberty will remain entire as regards points remaining outside the definitions. But these definitions will be the rule for all Catholics, and they should not disquiet anyone beforehand. Once more, they menace nothing that can with good reason be dear to you, men of this time, nothing but error and injustice, which are your enemies as well as ours. And if you would know the true thought of that magnanimous Pontiff, the object of so many odious and ungrateful calumnies, and of the Bishops, his sons and brothers; if you would imagine the spirit of the future Council, it is entirely in those beautiful words addressed by Pius IX. scarcely a year ago, to Catholic journalists, and inscribed by them, as a sacred device, upon their banner: "It is for Christian charity alone to clear the way, by getting rid of obstacles, to *that liberty*, *that fraternity* and *that progress*, of which souls are so ardently enamoured;" *Unius est caritatis iter sternere ad libertatem illam et fraternitatem et progressum, quorum desiderio tam acriter incenduntur animi.*

I cannot then too often repeat, and you cannot yourselves, my Brethren, repeat too often around you, that great is the error of those who denounce the future Council as a menace, as a work of war. We live in a time in which we are condemned to hear everything. But we should not let everything be believed. When already a year ago the Pope made known to the Bishops assembled at Rome his resolution to convoke an Œcumenical Council, what did the Bishops of the entire world see in that Council? A great work of illumination and pacification: *grande opus illuminationis et pacificationis;* these are the very terms of their Address. The Bull holds exactly the same language. In the Œcumenical Council what does the Pope ask his Brethren the Bishops, to examine, to inquire into with all possible care, and to decide with him? That which relates before all to the common peace and universal concord: *Ea omnia quæ communem omnium pacem et concordiam in primis respiciunt.*

This is the truth.

And when I re-read the Bull all through, in each page, in each line, what do I see? The expression of a solicitude, very worthy of the Father of souls, for civil Society no less than for the Church; he never separates them; he takes care to declare that their evils and their perils are common: *In sanctissimæ nostræ religionis civilisque societatis calamitatibus;* and that the same tempest beats one and the other with the same billows, *quâ tempestate nunc jactetur Ecclesia, et quibus quantisque malis civilis ipsa affligatur societas;* that at the present hour, and in this time which has been called transitional, both religion and society are passing through a formidable crisis, *non solum sanctissima nostra religio, verum etiam humana societas miserum in modum perturbatur ac vexatur;* that there are men to-day who would destroy the Church, if they could, and overthrow society itself even to its foundations, *ipsam Ecclesiam, si fieri unquam posset, et civilem societatem funditus evertere connituntur.* And it is to bring succour to one and the other, to conjure the perils which threaten then all at once, that the Holy Father has conceived the design of a Council; and the aim assigned by him to the Bishops, is precisely to sound this critical situation, and to bring the remedy to this double plague; "It is necessary," says he, "that our Venerable Brethren, who feel and deplore as we the critical situation of the Church and of Society, *una nobiscum tristissimam rei tum sacræ tum publicæ conditionem maxime dolentes,* apply themselves with Us with all their power to avert, by God's aid, from the Church and society, the evils which trouble them, *intentissimo studio curandum est ut, Deo bene juvante, omnia ab Ecclesiâ et civili societate amoveantur mala.*"

It is said that the Pope wishes to break with modern Society, to condemn, to proscribe it, to cast profound trouble on it; but never have the evils with which you suffer, Christian nations, more painfully moved the Head of the Church; never has he expressed himself in accents of more heartfelt sympathy for your perils and your griefs. And,—all the world has remarked it,—despoiled of three-quarters of his little State, reduced to Rome and the surrounding territory, placed between the perils of yesterday and those of to-morrow, suspended over abysses, the Pope does not appear pre-occupied therewith; it is not his threatened throne that he seeks to defend: not a phrase, not a word upon that great interest: no, in the Bull of Convocation, the temporal Prince forgets himself and is silent: the Pontiff alone has spoken to the world.

VII.

The Council and the Separated Churches.

We have not said all. One can conceive yet other hopes of the future Council. One loves to foresee in it other grand results. The letters of the Holy Father to the Eastern Bishops non-united, and to our separated Protestant brethren allow us to do so.

At two fatal epochs in the history of the world, two great divisions, my Brethren, have been made in that empire of souls, which is the Church; twice the seamless robe of Christ has been rent by schism and by heresy. These were the two misfortunes of mankind, and two of the real causes which have retarded the progress of the world.

Who knows not that if the old Greek Empire, if the East had not so sadly broken off with the West, it would never have been the prey of Islamism, which has so much debased it, and which yet to this day keeps it under its yoke; that it would not have gained over to the schism another vast empire, in whose bosom seventy millions of souls are groaning all at once under religious and political despotism?

And who can say what the Christian peoples of Europe would be to-day without Lutheranism, Calvinism, and so many other divisions, and how much these unfortunate separations have caused Christianity to lose of vital power for maintaining in the light of the Gospel so many souls, which incredulity has since led away from it? Who can say especially how the diffusion of the Gospel in infidel countries has been fettered by them?

Lamentable fact! There are still at this very hour millions of men upon whom the light of the Gospel has not dawned, and who are dwelling plunged in the darkness of infidelity. See those poor pagans upon the shores of their distant isles! They vaguely expect a Saviour; they extend their arms towards the true God; they appeal by the voice of their miseries and sufferings for light, truth and salvation. And it is eighteen centuries since Jesus Christ came to bring all this good to the world, and said to His Apostles these grand words: *Preach the Gospel to every creature!* Well! there were the Apostles of Jesus Christ, the disciples, the emulators of that Peter and that Paul who landed one day on the shores of Italy, who preached to our fathers the same Gospel, and died together for the same faith!

But, poor Indians, poor Japanese, after the apostles of the Catholic Church, sent by the successor of him to whom Jesus Christ said: "Thou art Peter, and upon this rock I will build my Church," other missionaries land who come to oppose them! Who sends them? Jesus Christ? What! Is Christ divided, as St. Paul asked with grief of the separatists of the first centuries? *Divisus est Christus?* Is not this, I ask you, O separated brethren, a frightful misfortune for those poor infidels? And is it not enough to cause every Christian heart to shed tears?

And would not union, if it were possible (and why should it not be, inasmuch as it is our Lord's will), now especially that all ways are open, and distances have vanished, be a happy and a great step towards that evangelization of every creature, the mission for which our Lord—on quitting this earth, confided to his apostles and their successors?

Yes, every soul, in which lives the Spirit of Jesus Christ, ought, as a martyr of the heart at sight of separations, to try and feel constrained to utter towards heaven the prayer of the Saviour, and the cry for unity: "That they may be one, as Thou, Father, art in Me, and I in Thee." Now, see the grand anticipation which rules the Head of the Catholic Church, when, forgetting his own perils, and moved by this solicitude for all the churches, which weighs upon him, *sollicitudo omnium Ecclesiarum*, he convokes the Œcumenical Council. He turns to the East and West, and addresses to all the separated communions a word of peace, a generous call to unity; whatever may be the reception given to his words, who would not perceive in this supreme effort for the union of all Christians a thought from heaven, inspired by Him who willed that His Church should be one and who said, as the Holy Father has been pleased to call to mind, "By this shall all men know that you are my disciples."

Will our brethren of the East and West respond to this thought, to this wish?

The East! What, not to be moved before that cradle of the ancient faith, from whence light has come to us! I have seen the Catholic Bishops of the East thrill at the announcement of the future Council, and fondly hope for their churches a revival of new life and fruitful activity.

But would the disunited Eastern Churches refuse to hear those "words of peace and charity" that the Holy Father has just addressed to them "with all the effusion of his heart?"* Why should they be deaf to this appeal? For what antiquated or chimerical fears?

Who has not noticed, and who has not been deeply touched by, the delicacy, and the accent of particular

* Apostolic Letter of His Holiness Pius IX to all the Bishops of the churches of the Oriental rite, who are not in communion with the Holy Apostolic See, dated 8 Sept., 1868.

tenderness with which the Holy Father speaks to our Oriental brethren, who, in the midst of that Mahometan Asia, "acknowledge and adore Jesus Christ, as we; and who, redeemed by His most precious blood, have been admitted by holy baptism to His Church!" What regard for those ancient Churches, to-day so unfortunately separated from unity, but who, formerly, "shed such lustre by their sanctity and heavenly doctrine, and yielded abundant fruit for the glory of God and the salvation of souls."*

And at the same time, what gentleness, what forgetfulness of all his irritating griefs! The Holy Father speaks but of charity and peace; he asks only one thing, which is, that "the ancient laws of love being renewed, and the peace of our fathers, that salutary and heavenly gift from Christ, disappeared for a time, being solidly re-established, the serene light of a desired union may shine before the eyes of all after the clouds of a long mourning, and the sombre and gloomy obscurity of long disagreements."*

Why should not this desire for union and peace, so deep in the heart not only of the Holy Father, but also, let not our Oriental brethren doubt, in the hearts of all the Bishops and all the Christians of the West, be the hearts' desire of them also, and of whomsoever bears the name of Christian upon the earth? My God! is there, then, good in this rending of Christ's robe? And what, I ask them, do the Churches of the ancient East gain in light and in charity by not communicating with those of the whole universe? Who hinders them? Are we, then, still in the times of the metaphysical subtleties and cavils of the *Bas*-Empire?

I was speaking just now of infidel nations: perhaps our brethren, the Oriental Bishops, will permit me to remind them here of what is at this moment the state of the entire world, and the situation of the Church of Jesus Christ over the whole world. If at all times the Church had to struggle, is she not at this moment

---

* *Ibidem.*

more than ever combated and harassed? Does not the spirit, unfortunately impious, of revolution rise up against her from all sides? And you, Oriental Churches, united or not, have you not also your perils? Is not your spiritual liberty being made prey of unceasingly? Is not with you Christianity surrounded by eager enemies, on the right, on the left, on all sides? And does not even the wind of impiety, which agitates Europe, now that distances no longer exist, blow also to Asia, and are those believing races of the ancient East itself, under the repeated efforts of an irreligious press, quite sure of never being hit?

In a position so serious, and which has happened everywhere to the Church of Jesus Christ by reason of the misfortunes of the times, is it not all Christians' first want to put an end to discords which are enfeebling, and to seek in reconciliation and peace unity, which is strength? What Bishop, what true Christian, meditating before God upon these things, would say: No, division is good; unity would be a misfortune! Who does not perceive on the contrary that union, that the return to unity, is a certain benefit for souls, the manifest will of God, and that it would be the salvation of your Churches? What? There are personal considerations, certain human motives, superior to these great interests and great duties? Did your fathers, those illustrious doctors, the Athanasiuses, the Gregorys Nazianzen, the Basils, the Cyrils, the Chrysostoms, make any difficulty in bending their glorious heads before him whom they call "the firm and solid rock upon which the Saviour has built His Church"?* If they were living to-day, would they not christianly and nobly tread under foot an independence which is not according to Christ, together with all the suggestions of blinded pride? If past centuries have committed a fault, must it be eternal?

* *Ibidem.* The words of St. Gregory Nazianzen, quoted by the Holy Father.

But does not time, if you hearken to its lessons, O Eastern brethren, convey to you here serious instruction? Cannot you, who are surrounded by despotism on the one hand, and Islamism on the other, cannot you feel in fact the perils of isolation and the fatal consequences of the rupture?

God preserve me from any word which might be ever so little painful to you, coming as I do at this moment with all the charity of Jesus Christ!

But, whether I think of those unhappy populations, whose souls and whose land have become sterile under the yoke of the religion of Mahomet; or whether I cast a look towards those Russian populations so religious and steady in their morals, and who dwell in the faith of Jesus Christ in spite of the abasement of their churches, and notwithstanding the supremacy of a Czar, whose pretended orthodoxy does not inspire even a little justice and pity for Poland, I feel my heart deeply moved, and I pray for so many peoples worthy of such profound interest, such great compassion.

O separated brethren of the East, Greeks, Syrians, Armenians, Chaldeans, Bulgarians, Russians, Sclavonians, and all you whom I cannot name, see, the Catholic Church comes to you, and stretches out to you her arms. O our brethren, come!

She wishes to assemble all entire: from all parts of the inhabited world, from our West, from your East, from the New World also and from distant islands, her Bishops wish to hasten, at the voice of the Supreme Head, to Rome, to the centre of unity. Ah, well, she wishes not to assemble without you. O our brethren, come!

Here is one of those solemn and rare occasions, to meet with the like of which requires centuries. The Catholic Church offers you peace: "We pray you with all our strength," writes the Holy Father, "We press you to come to this general Synod, as your ancestors came to the Council of Lyons and to the Council of Florence, in order to renew union and peace."* Would you on your side refuse to make a-

* *Ibidem.*

single step towards us, and would you thus let slip so favourable a circumstance? Who, then, would take upon himself such a terrible responsibility? O our brethren, come!

The heart of the Church of Jesus Christ changes not: but times have changed, and the causes which made the efforts attempted by our fathers so sadly fail, thank God, no longer exist. O all of you, O our brethren, come at last!

For ourselves, we are full of hope, and whatever may be the resistance which the surprise of the first moment perhaps, or antique prejudices have roused, all of us appear prepared for many reconciliations. "Rome," cried out Bossuet formerly, "ceases not to cry to the most distant peoples, in order to call them to the banquet, where all are made one; and see how at this maternal voice the extremities of the East are shaken, and how they seem to wish to give birth to a new Christianity!"

O God! that we could see this spectacle! What joy for Thy Church upon earth, in the midst of so many sharp struggles and bitter griefs! What joy also for the Church in heaven, and particularly, O Churches of the East, for your Saints and your Doctors, "when," as the Holy Father says, "above in heaven, they shall see union re-established with the Apostolic See, the centre of Catholic truth and unity; that union which, during their life here below, they laboured to revive, to propagate by all their studies and indefatigable toil, by doctrine and by example, enflamed as they were by that charity, infused into their hearts by the Holy Spirit, for Him who willed that the mark of his disciples should be unity, and who addressed this prayer to his Father: 'That they may be one, as we also are one!'"†

Oh, mark well the language of the Church, the true Church of Jesus Christ, which alone amongst all Chris-

† *Ibidem.* Unity will eternally be the character of the true Church. All questions on the Church will ever be reduced principally to this question: "*Where is unity?*"

tian societies, utters a maternal cry, and demands all her children, because she is the true Mother!

And this is also why the Sovereign Pontiff, after having turned towards the separated East, turns about towards the other Christian communions non-Catholic, and addresses to all our brethren of Protestantism the same pressing appeal.

Protestantism! "Ah!" cried out again Bossuet, in his ardent love, in his passionate longing for unity, "Our bowels are moved at that name, and the Church, ever a mother, at this remembrance cannot help renewing her lamentations and her desires."

These are the lamentations and desires that the Holy Father has caused to be heard anew, in that apostolic letter, addressed some days after the Brief for the Oriental Bishops "to all Protestants and other non-Catholics," and in which, after having deplored the misfortunes of division, and pointed out the great benefits of that unity willed by our Saviour, he exhorts, he supplicates all Christians separated from him to return to the fold of Jesus Christ. "In all our prayers and supplications," he continues, "we never cease day and night humbly to ask for them, of the Eternal Pastor of Souls, heavenly light and abundance of grace, and we await with open arms the return of our erring children."*

This is what the Holy Father says, and with him the whole Church. Ah, well! shall we hope, and shall we pray always in vain, and will then the work of return be as difficult as many think?

Prejudice, I know, is still strong; and the difficulty which in noble England encounters the work of tardy justice, which has just been commenced, is one among many other proofs of this; but it is precisely the Council which here can still clear up misunderstandings, and by appeasing the heart prepare the return of the mind.

And to him who might be tempted to accuse me of delusion, I would reply, that amongst those of our

* Apostolic Letter of the 13th Sept., 1868.

separated brethren whom the sad course of rationalism does not affect, the number of souls who deplore the rupture of unity becomes greater every day. I call England, I call America to witness this: I would answer that, more than once, I myself have received painful confidences, and heard suffering hearts call with deep lamentations, as we, for the day when shall be accomplished that saying of the Master: *Unum Ovile et unus Pastor*. Is it, then, said that that day will never arrive? Are separations necessary? and why should we not be destined to see the times foreseen and greeted by Bossuet?

Here, no doubt, the dogmatical difficulties are serious; but they would disappear if one removes that which to me is the most serious of all, viz., the denial of all doctrinal authority in the Church, the absolute liberty of conscience which confounds itself, whether one will or not, with the principle even of rationalism. Hence, in effect, Protestantism bears in its heart the original vice of a radical inconsistency, which the most enlightened and firm minds amongst our separated brethren are deploring; and therefore our hope is at least for numerous individual conversions, and, perhaps, may God so will! for greater reconciliations.

This capital point settled—and its settlement is easy to simple good sense and courageous good faith—all the rest vanishes. Reason says with evidence that Jesus Christ could have not wished to constitute His Church without this essential principle of stability and unity, under pain of founding a Christianity incapable of enduring and being perpetuated like Himself—a religion given up as a prey to all the mobilities of individual interpretations. This is evident of itself, independent of any text.

But there are texts which, for right minds, and without great disputes, equally gain over everything. I will recall but three of them; the first is: *Tu es Petrus*, Thou art Peter—the primacy of St. Peter and the Head of the Church; the second is: *Hoc est corpus meum*, This is my Body—the Eucharist; the third is:

Ecce Mater tua, Behold thy Mother—the Blessed Virgin. Have you been able to efface from the Gospel those three sentences ! Have you meditated sufficiently upon them, and so many others no less decisive ?

From the Gospel pass to History, and from texts pass to facts.

Do not facts loudly tell you that the living element of complete Christianity is wanting in you ? For, on the one side, you have had time to know thoroughly the authors of the rupture, and on the other, you have been able to consider its consequences. For three centuries you have been in the face of the Gospel ; for three centuries you have been in the face of History. Now, have not these three centuries, which have slipped away, brought you new and serious instruction upon this capital point ? The principle of Protestantism, in developing itself, has borne its fruits, and the foresight of the Catholic doctors in the old controversies is realized every day before your eyes. Contemporary Protestantism goes on more and more dissolving into rationalism ; many of its ministers, they proclaim it themselves, have no longer supernatural faith, and lately a cry of alarm, proceeding from her bosom, has resounded in our political assemblies ; but a cry lost in the air ! Dissolution will continue, in spite of noble efforts and christian resistance, to become ever greater, and to ruin more and more that incomplete Christianity, in which is wanting the essential power which preserves and defends authority. To lose Christianity in pure philosophy, is, whether one will or not, to what modern Protestantism tends. But from the excess of evil good may proceed ; and what more proper to enlighten upon the radical vice of the Protestant Churches the souls seduced, but honest, who would fain remain christian, than that spectacle of decomposition, in view of the powerful unity of the Catholic Church and of the Council, which is about to be the living manifestation thereof ?

There is another hope, less in accord, I am convinced, with human probabilities, but which my faith in the Divine Mercy does not forbid me to conceive ; it is, that the Jews themselves, the children of Israel, who, mingled with us, live to-day in our social life, will feel something that will move their hearts, and lead them, docile at last at the voice of St. Paul, to the bosom of the Church. In the Jews, in fact, so visibly, so long punished, I cannot but recognize my forefathers in the faith, the children of Moses, the fellow-countrymen of Joseph and Mary, of Peter and Paul, those of whom the latter said: "To whom belongeth the adoption *as* of children, and the glory and the testament, and the giving of the law, and the service *of God*, and the promises: whose are the fathers, and of whom is Christ, according to the flesh, who is over all things, God blessed for ever." *Quorum adoptio est filiorum, et gloria, et testamentum et legislatio, et promissa, quorum patres, et ex quibus Christus secundum carnem, qui est super omnia Deus benedictus in sæcula.** I beseech them then to believe in Him whom they expect; I beseech them to believe in eighteen hundred years of history, for history, as a fifth Gospel, proves the coming and the Divinity of the Messias.

Do not wonder, my Brethren, if I feel full of compassion for Protestants, Greeks and Jews, whilst people accuse me of being hard upon the inventors of modern incredulity. I know how to distinguish between errors which commence, and errors which finish, between the responsible, culpable authors, who disseminate error knowingly, and the innocent victims, in good faith, who after centuries remain attached thereto. How could I but feel moved to tears on seeing those populations of my country, those workmen, those peasants, so laborious and so worthy of all our sympathies, those young people in our schools whose ardent spirit sighs for truth, and who fall, before they are cognizant of it themselves, into the hands of the masters of error? When, some years ago, the revival of faith was so sensible, and a decided progress towards good seemed to have been made, all of a sudden shades gather around, abysses open, the breath of an impious science and a

* Romans ix. 4, 5.

violent press becomes stronger, and that beautiful vessel of faith and French prosperity threatens to sink while leaving the port! Ah! I execrate the authors of so cruel a shipwreck, whilst I feel full of pity for so many sincere souls whom I see among our separated brethren, born in error, but who caused not its birth! With what ardour do I extend towards these captive souls my brotherly arms! May they return to the Church; for she it is who preserves for them Jesus Christ, God of the whole Truth, and invites them to that great banquet of the father of the family, where, as Bossuet so well said, "All are made one."

May the next Council, the work of pacification and light, draw to us at last so many souls who already belong to us by their sincerity, their virtues, and, I know it of many, by their wishes! May this be, at least, my Brethren, the desire of all Catholics! Yes, let us open our hearts to all these well-beloved brothers with more effusion than ever; let us wish, as the Holy Father desires, that the future Council may be a powerful and happy effort towards union, and let us cause to ascend unceasingly towards heaven that prayer of the Master: *Sint unum, sicut et nos!*

VIII.

The Catholic Church.

O you, to whom the duties of my charge oblige me to address myself obstinately, "in season or out of season," as St. Paul said, sometimes with austere words upon the lips, but ever with charity in the heart, adversaries of my faith, whoever you are, philosophers, Protestants, indifferent men, and I would that my words could travel even to you also, poor pagans, lost in the darkness of the superstitions which still cover half the globe! O my brothers, would that I could make you taste, for a single instant, the profound peace that one experiences in living and dying in the arms of the Holy Catholic Church! Be my witnesses, you who are my brothers in the Priesthood, and you, faithful Christians, of every rank, of every sex, of every age! When one feels oneself surrounded by this light; assured by these hopes, preceded by those sublime creatures who are called Saints, whose glory in Heaven the Church upon earth to-day salutes, connected with the tradition of all Christian ages by the successors of the Apostles, and founded, lastly, upon Jesus Christ, what joy! what company! what strength and what repose in the certainty and the light!

I am convinced, and every day brings me the proof, that, hearing the cries which are raised against us, you would believe that people detest us. Well, no, the dominant feeling with our enemies is not always hate. There is another, which they do not avow, but which is more frequent with them; it is envy. Yes, they envy us sometimes, and the Atheist says secretly to himself, at the moment even when he insults a Christian: "How happy he is!"

Do not believe, my Brethren, what you hear said of the Church, that her august countenance is for ever disfigured by calumny, and that men are beginning to see nothing more in her than a mistress of tyranny and ignorance. Those violent prejudices have assuredly some force; our enemies and our faults are answerable for propagating them. But the Church, in spite of all that, and the Œcumenical Council will soon give a new proof of it to the world, does not the less remain the Spouse of Christ, without stain and without blemish, notwithstanding the weakness of her children, and there is not one of those who attack her that could say, little that he may have of good faith, what evil the Church has done him! *Popule meus, quid feci tibi?*

What evil! Inhabitants of town and country, you owe to her the purity of your children, the fidelity of your wives, the probity of your neighbours, the justice of your laws, the festivals in your monotonous lives, a little art in the midst of your little dwellings, and hope beyond the cemetery and the tomb.

This is the evil she has done you, this enemy of the human race!

And if you can rise above yourself, beyond your interests, beyond your hamlet, and if your thoughts soar a little higher than the smoke which issues from your roofs, what a spectacle is offered to your view by the Catholic Church, already so great, so good, in the little history of each one of us; greater and more beneficent in the history of the laborious developments of human society!

The inseparable companion of man upon earth, she suffers, she strives with him; she has assisted, inspired and guided mankind in all its most painful and most glorious transformations.

She it is who has caused to issue, even from the midst of pagan corruption, virtues, whose name even the earth knew not, and souls of such purity, elevation, and nobility that the world yet to-day falls upon its knees before them!

She it is who has subdued and transformed barbarians, and who, during the long and perilous travail of modern society in the Middle Ages, has courageously combated evil, and presided over all progress.

She it is, ungrateful modern society, who will still aid you to-day, if you do not break with her, to disengage, in the midst of all those confused elements which agitate themselves within you, the germs of life from the principles of death, by maintaining unshaken the truths which alone can save you.

Ah! my Brethren, we do not enough know what the Catholic Church is! We live in the midst of her, we make a part of her, and we know her not. We ignore both what she was and what she is in the world, the mission that God has given her, and the living power, the divine privileges deposited in her, in order that she may be able to accomplish eternally her task upon earth, maintain immutable here below truth and good, light and virtue, and remain always, as the Apostle says, *Ecclesia columna et firmamentum veritatis.*

Surely I have never heard of reproaching a pillar for being immovable: what would become of the edifice if the pillar stirred? Why then do you reproach the Church for being immovable, and how is this immobility not salutary to you? Where would you be if there were quakings of the truth as there are quakings of the earth? Whilst you scatter, we unite. Whilst you lose, we keep. We can say to doctrines: "We have known at Alexandria or at Athens, you, your mothers, your daughters and your relations." The Church can say to the nations whose ambassadors the Pope assembles: "France, thou has been formed by my Bishops, whose names thy streets and thy villages bear! England, who has then made thee, and why hast thou been called the Isle of Saints? Germany, thou hast entered into the civilization of the West by my envoy St. Boniface; Russia, where wouldst thou be, without my Cyril and my Methodius? Kings, I have known your ancestors. Before the Hapsbourgs, the Bourbons, the Romanoffs, the Brunswicks, the Hohenzollerns, the Bonapartes, and the Carignans, I was ancient, and I have seen the Cæsars and the Antoninuses die. To-morrow I shall be still the same." Without money, without dwelling, without power, say you? "That may be, and I have a hundred times experienced these trials, being always ready to address to nations that little saying of Jesus to Zacheus: 'My friend, this day I must abide in thy house.' If I quit Rome for a moment, I shall dwell in London, Paris or New York." It is only the Church and the sun who could affirm with certainty that the next day, without fail, we shall see them rise; and this is what the Church does in daring, amidst the tumult of the present hour, to announce a Council.

Admirable spectacle, which our century would wish not to admire, but whose grandeur it is constrained to acknowledge! Yes, weary looks rest themselves with irresistible emotion upon that majestic pillar, alone standing midst the ruins of the past and the actual levelling of all human greatness. Indifferent persons themselves feel troubled, surprised, attracted at the sight of that Church attesting by so great an act her immortal power; and after having exhausted all doctrines, more than one is tempted to say to the Supreme Pontiff what St. Peter, the first Pontiff, said to Jesus: "Master, to whom should we go? Thou hast the words of eternal life!"

Hear those words of life, ye who doubt, ye who seek, ye who suffer! Hear them also, ye who triumph, ye who rejoice, ye who oppress men! Hear the words that the Catholic Church causes to be simply repeated, at each rising of the sun, by little children:

Credo, I believe! I believe in one God, the Creator. Behold, scholars, the answer to your uncertainties.

Credo, I believe! I believe in a Saviour of the world, who by His Birth has consecrated purity, by His Precepts confounded pride, by His Sufferings dishonoured injustice, by His Resurrection proved His Divinity and our Immortality! I believe in Jesus Christ! Behold, poor afflicted people, poor oppressed nations, the answer to your despairs!

Credo, I believe! I believe in the Holy Ghost, in the Holy Catholic Church, in the communion of the just, living and dead, in the remission of sins, in the judgment, and in the happy life of all those who have fought the good fight. Behold, Protestants or philosophers, so divided in your affirmations, so limited in your hopes, the response to your quarrels! Behold, oppressing potentates, the response to your iniquities! And behold, also, O pitiless death, the response to thy rigours!

Loving, hoping, believing! All there; and it is the Church who alone preserves to men these treasures in the unshaken majesty and universal truth of that Credo, which the Nineteenth Council, at the dawn of the twentieth century, is preparing to re-say with the two-hundred and sixty-second successor of Peter, the fisherman, Jesus Christ's first Apostle.

But let us cease to speak, my Brethren, let us cease to dispute, cease to fear, and, bending the knee, let us pray.

O God, who knowest the secrets of thy Providence, and

the marvels that the Church can yet show to the world, if the passions and faults of men thwart them not!

O God, if religion and society, supported one upon the other, would pursue with common consent their beneficent way, what a great step towards the establishment of Thy kingdom upon earth, towards the true progress of nations, towards liberty by the truth, towards the true brotherhood of men, towards the extinction of revolutions and wars, towards the peace of the world!

Ah! a new era would commence, and a new and great age appear in history.

Let us open our hearts to these hopes; let us ask of God true good, and let us only foresee possible evil in order to prevent it. Let people know, at least, that Catholics are not men of discouragement, nor of sinister predictions, nor of irritating defiance, but men of charity, of noble hopes, of peaceful efforts, as at the same time of generous strife.

Let us invoke SS. Peter and Paul, let us invoke the Blessed Virgin Mary, Mother of Jesus, the glory and heavenly Patroness of the family of men; and, united to the souls of all the Saints, let us pray to the Adorable Trinity reigning in Heaven!

Let us pray, in order that the Council may accomplish its work! that Christian nations may not repulse that supreme effort by which the Church endeavours to succour them! that light may enter their minds, and that hearts may be appeased! that misunderstandings may be cleared up, that prejudices may be removed, that causeless griefs may disappear, that a new efflorescence of Christianity, and consequently of civilization, may be caused in the world, and that the reconciliations so desired and so necessary may be accomplished!

Let us pray that Sovereigns, according to the wish and the formal demand which the Holy Father addresses to them, abjuring all vain suspicions, may favour, by the liberty of the Bishops, the future Assembly of the Church, and permit her to hold her Council in peace.

Let us pray that nations also, comprehending the maternal intentions of the Church, and closing their ears to calumnies, may hear with confidence and accept with docility the word of their Mother.

Let us pray that her declared adversaries themselves may make a truce to their suspicions, to their anger, at least until in her Council and under the inspiration of the Holy Spirit, she has issued decrees whose wisdom and charity will touch them.

Let us pray that so many men of integrity, scholars, politicians, heads of families, so many men of toil, so many men of good-will, whom the light of Jesus Christ has not yet illumined, may receive from it beneficent rays.

Let us pray that the restless desires of so many mothers, sisters, wives, daughters, who in obscurity maintain purity and sanctity in the family, often without being able to obtain the faith, may at length be favourably heard.

Let us pray that at last the East and the West may draw near, and that our separated brethren, weary of the division which dissolves them, may respond to the pressing appeal that Holy Church has made to them, and come at length to throw themselves into her arms, open for three centuries.

Let us pray that the Church, in her faithful, in her Ministers, may each day be more pure, more pious, more learned, more charitable, in order that our faults, my Brethren, may not be an obstacle to the Kingdom of God, which we are charged to make loved.

Finally, let us pray for the Holy Father. Vouchsafe, O God, to preserve him to Thy Church, and grant that this great Pontiff who fears not, in spite of the weariness of age, to undertake the laborious work of a Council, may also see its happy issue. Grant that, after so many trials, so firmly borne, he may finally rejoice in the triumph of the Church, before going to receive in heaven the recompense for his labours and his virtues!

ORLEANS,
1st *November*, 1868.

FELIX,
BISHOP OF ORLEANS.

BIBLIOTHEQUE DE PREDICATEURS.

PUBLICATIONS NOUVELLES POUR 1869.

VIES DES SAINTS A L'USAGE DES PREDICATEURS. 4 vols., 24 fr. (19/3)—T. 1er, contenant: Janvier, Février, et Mars, 6 fr. (4/10)—T. II, contenant: Avril, Mai, et Juin, 6 fr. (4/10)—T. III, contenant; Juillet, Août, et Septembre, 6 fr. (4/10)—T. IV, contenant: Octobre, Novembre, et Décembre, 6 fr. (4/10).

DICTIONNAIRE DE PREDICATION, ancienne, moderne, et contemporaine. 10 vols., 40 fr. (32/-).

CALENDRIER DES PREDICATEURS, ou INDICATEUR: 1° des sujets de *Predication* relatifs à l'Épitre, à l'Evangile de chaque dimanche, aux Fêtes de chaque jour. au Propre du temps, aux circonstances; 2° des *Plans* de ces sujets; 3° des *Sources* où l'on peut puiser pour leur composition ou leur improvisation. 5 fr. (4/-)

PANORAMA DES PREDICATEURS. 3 vols., 30 fr. (24/-).

REPERTOIRE DE LA DOCTRINE CHRETIENNE. 3 vols., 18 fr. (14/5). T. 1er, *Symbole*, 6 fr. (4/10); T II, *Décalogue*, 6 fr. (4/10); T. III, *Sacrements*, 6 fr. (4/10).

ANNEE PASTORALE, ou Cours complet de Sermons populaires, de Prônes, et d'Homélies sur l'Evangile de chaque dimanche de l'année. vols., 12 fr. (9/8).

SERMONS NOUVEAUX ET COMPLETS SUR LES MYSTERES DE N. S. JESUS CHRIST. 2 vols., 12 fr. (9/8).

RETRAITES: (chaque volume 1 fr. 50) (1/3).

- 1re Série—Sermons des meilleurs Prédicateurs contemporains pour Missions, Retraites, Jubilé, Stations de pénitence.
- 2e ,, Sermons de plus célèbres Prédicateurs contemporains pour une Retraite spéciale d'hommes.
- 3e ,, Sermons des plus célèbres Prédicateurs contemporains pour une Retraite spéciale de femmes.
- 4e ,, Sermons, Instructions et Indications pour une Retraite de première communion.
- 5e ,, Sermons et Instructions pour une Retraite de jeunes personnes.
- 6e ,, Sermons de nos célèbres Prédicateurs contemporains pour le *Triduum* de l'Adoration perpétuelle du T.-S. Sacrement.

SERMONS D'ACTUALITE SUR L'EGLISE. 2 fr. (1/7).

LE REVUE MENSUELLE, Recueils de Prônes, Instructions, Conférences, Panégyriques, pour tous les Dimanches et toutes les Fêtes de l'année. Depuis 1857. Chaque année est indépendante et différente d'une autre et se vend séparément au de prix de 4 fr. (3/3).

MOIS DE MARIE DES PREDICATEURS. 2 vols., 12 fr. (9/8).

PORTRAITS LITTERAIRES DES PLUS CELEBRES PREDICATEURS CONTEMPORAINS. 2 fr. (1/7.)

R. WASHBOURNE, 18A, *Paternoster Row, London.*

www.ingramcontent.com/pod-product-compliance
Lightning Source LLC
Chambersburg PA
CBHW021519090426
42739CB00007B/691

9783337125271